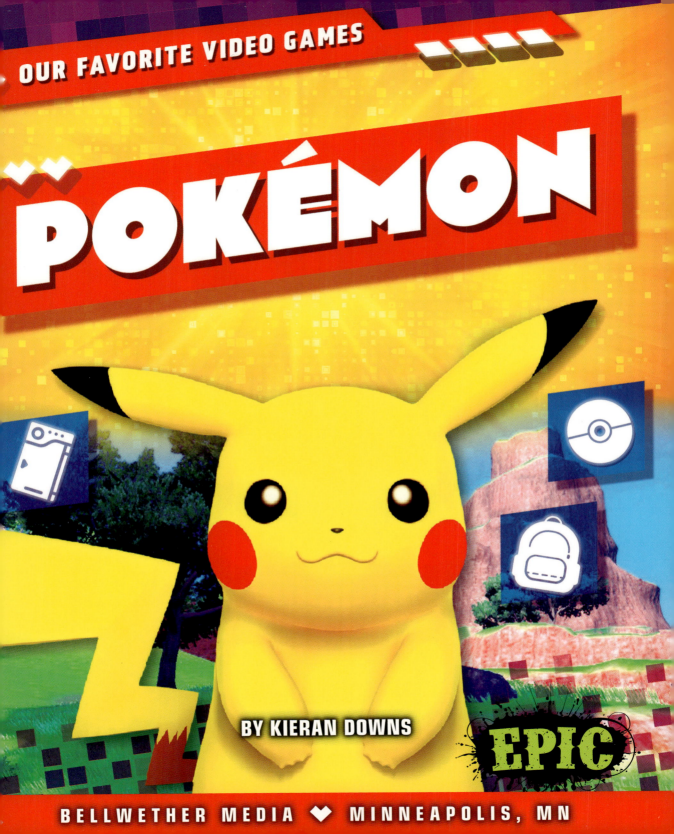

EPIC BOOKS are no ordinary books. They burst with intense action, high-speed heroics, and shadows of the unknown. Are you ready for an Epic adventure?

This is not an official Pokémon book. It is not approved by or connected with The Pokémon Company.

This edition first published in 2025 by Bellwether Media, Inc.

No part of this publication may be reproduced in whole or in part without written permission of the publisher. For information regarding permission, write to Bellwether Media, Inc., Attention: Permissions Department, 6012 Blue Circle Drive, Minnetonka, MN 55343.

Library of Congress Cataloging-in-Publication Data

Names: Downs, Kieran, author.
Title: Pokémon / by Kieran Downs.
Description: Minneapolis, MN : Bellwether Media, 2025. | Series: Epic. Our favorite video games | Includes bibliographical references and index. | Audience: Ages 7-12 | Audience: Grades 2-3 | Summary: "Engaging images accompany information about Pokémon. The combination of high-interest subject matter and light text is intended for students in grades 2 through 7"-- Provided by publisher.
Identifiers: LCCN 2024005432 (print) | LCCN 2024005433 (ebook) | ISBN 9798893040487 (library binding) | ISBN 9781644879887 (ebook)
Subjects: LCSH: Pokémon (Game)--Juvenile literature.
Classification: LCC GV1469.35.P63 D68 2025 (print) | LCC GV1469.35.P63 (ebook) | DDC 794.8--dc23/eng/20240205
LC record available at https://lccn.loc.gov/2024005432
LC ebook record available at https://lccn.loc.gov/2024005433

Text copyright © 2025 by Bellwether Media, Inc. EPIC and associated logos are trademarks and/or registered trademarks of Bellwether Media, Inc. Bellwether Media is a division of Chrysalis Education Group.

Editor: Elizabeth Neuenfeldt   Designer: Gabriel Hilger

Printed in the United States of America, North Mankato, MN.

TABLE OF CONTENTS

GOTTA CATCH 'EM ALL	4
THE HISTORY OF POKÉMON	8
POKÉMON TODAY	16
POKÉMON FANS	20
GLOSSARY	22
TO LEARN MORE	23
INDEX	24

000
HIGH SCORE

GOTTA CATCH 'EM ALL

A player looks for Pokémon in *Pokémon Violet*. They spot one hiding in the grass. They send out their own Pokémon to battle it!

Then the player throws a Poké Ball. They catch the Pokémon!

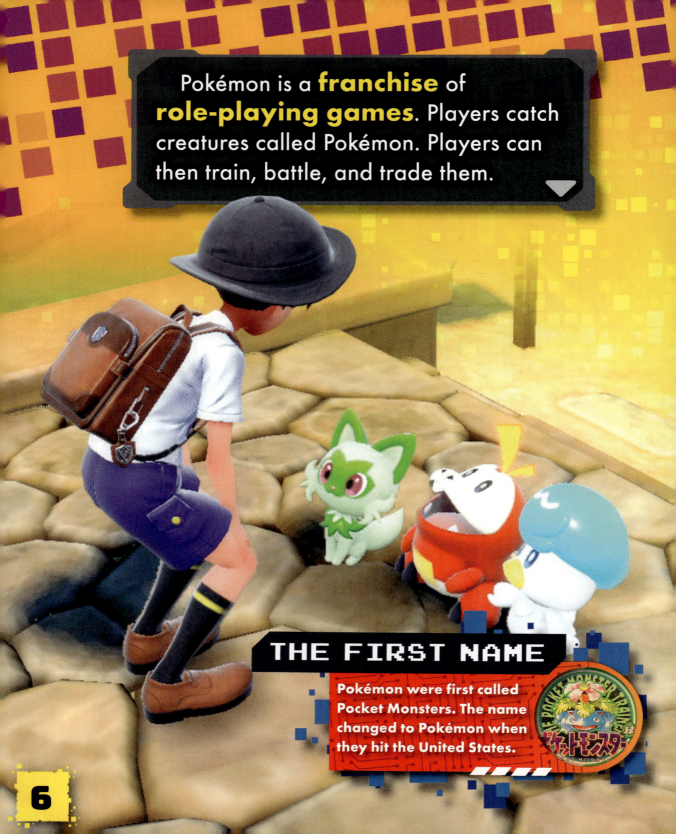

Pokémon is a **franchise** of **role-playing games**. Players catch creatures called Pokémon. Players can then train, battle, and trade them.

THE FIRST NAME

Pokémon were first called Pocket Monsters. The name changed to Pokémon when they hit the United States.

FIRST STARTER POKÉMON

BULBASAUR

CHARMANDER

SQUIRTLE

> Players can play Pokémon alone or with friends. They can battle and trade online.

THE HISTORY OF POKÉMON

SATOSHI TAJIRI

Pokémon was created by Satoshi Tajiri. He was **inspired** by looking for bugs as a child.

Game Freak released *Pokémon Red* and *Green* in Japan in 1996. They were made for the Nintendo Game Boy. They were a hit!

GAME BOY

DEVELOPER PROFILE

NAME	Game Freak
LOCATION	Tokyo, Japan
YEAR FOUNDED	1989
NUMBER OF EMPLOYEES	more than 150

In 1998, *Pokémon Red* and *Green* came to the United States. They were renamed *Pokémon Red* and *Blue*.

POKÉMON RED

A LOT OF POKEMON

Pokémon Red and *Blue* had 151 different Pokémon. Today there are over 1,000 different Pokémon!

Later, *Pokémon Gold* and *Silver* came out for the Game Boy Color. They were **sequels** to *Red* and *Blue*!

In 2006, *Pokémon Diamond* and *Pearl* first came out in Japan. These Nintendo DS games let players trade and battle online!

In 2013, *Pokémon X* and *Y* came out on the Nintendo 3DS. They were the first **3D** Pokémon games!

POKÉMON SWORD

POKÉMON VIOLET

In 2019, *Pokémon Sword* and *Shield* came out on the Nintendo Switch. They were a hit!

Pokémon Scarlet and *Violet* came out in 2022. They were the first **open-world** Pokémon games.

POKÉMON TIMELINE

1996

Pokémon Red and *Green* come out in Japan

1998

Pokémon Red and *Blue* come out in the U.S.

2006

Pokémon Diamond and *Pearl* allow players to play online

2019

Pokémon Sword and *Shield* come out on the Nintendo Switch

2022

Pokémon Scarlet and *Violet* are the first open-world Pokémon games

POKÉMON TODAY

Pokémon games today are played on **consoles** and **smartphones**. Players explore 3D areas looking for Pokémon.

POKÉMON GAMES BY SALES

Players battle against other **trainers**. They battle strong trainers called gym leaders.

17

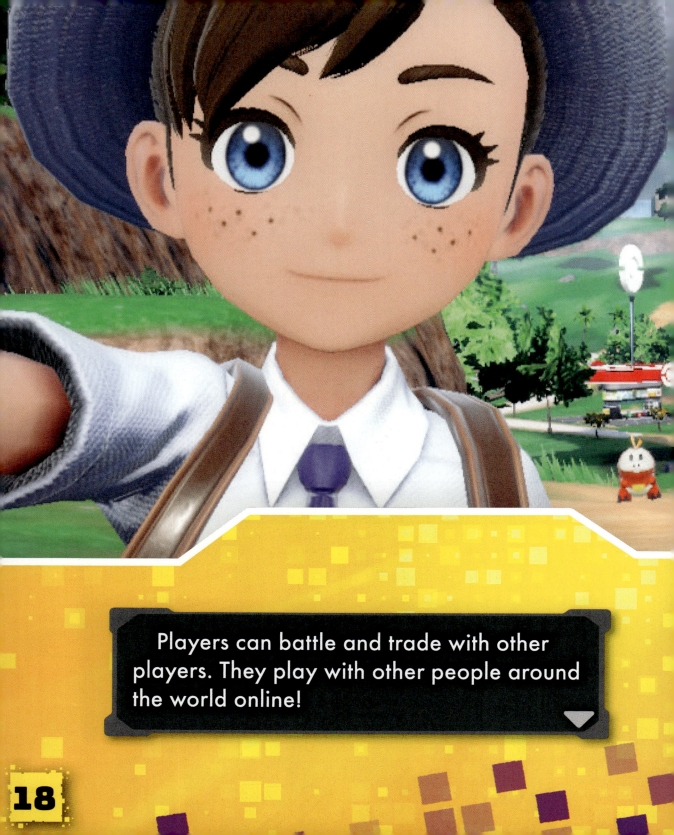

Players can battle and trade with other players. They play with other people around the world online!

ON THE GO

In 2016, *Pokémon GO* was made for smartphones. Players could find Pokémon in the real world!

Players can do special battles called raids. They work with other players to catch tough Pokémon.

POKÉMON FANS

Pokémon fans can watch Pokémon movies and TV shows. Many people collect Pokémon trading cards. The Pokémon World **Championships** happen every year. Trainers can show they are the very best!

POKÉMON WORLD CHAMPIONSHIPS

DATE once a year

LOCATION around the world

EVENT a big championship for many kinds of Pokémon games

20

GLOSSARY

3D—related to something that has height, width, and depth; players can move in any direction in a 3D game.

championships—contests to decide the best team or person

consoles—game systems that connect to screens to play video games

franchise—a series of related works that take place in the same world

inspired—given an idea about what to do or create

open-world—related to a game where players explore a wide area at their own pace

role-playing games—games in which players take on the role of their characters

sequels—works that continue the story of a previous work

smartphones—cell phones with advanced features such as internet access and apps

trainers—people who train, battle, and trade Pokémon

TO LEARN MORE

AT THE LIBRARY

Hansen, Grace. *Pokémon.* Minneapolis, Minn.: Abdo Kids, 2023.

Neuenfeldt, Elizabeth. *Video Games.* Minneapolis, Minn.: Bellwether Media, 2023.

Rathburn, Betsy. *Video Game Developer.* Minneapolis, Minn.: Bellwether Media, 2023.

ON THE WEB

Factsurfer.com gives you a safe, fun way to find more information.

1. Go to www.factsurfer.com.

2. Enter "Pokémon" into the search box and click 🔍.

3. Select your book cover to see a list of related content.

INDEX

3D, 13, 16

battle, 4, 6, 7, 12, 17, 18, 19

consoles, 9, 11, 12, 13, 14, 16

fans, 20

first starter Pokémon, 7

Game Freak, 9

history, 8, 9, 10, 11, 12, 13, 14, 15, 19

Japan, 9, 12

movies, 20, 21

name, 6, 10

online, 12, 18

open-world games, 14

players, 4, 6, 7, 12, 16, 17, 18, 19

Poké Ball, 4

Pokémon, 4, 6, 7, 11, 16, 19

Pokémon Diamond and *Pearl*, 12

Pokémon GO, 19

Pokémon Gold and *Silver*, 11

Pokémon Red, Green, and Blue, 9, 10, 11

Pokémon Scarlet and *Violet*, 4, 5, 14

Pokémon Sword and *Shield*, 14

Pokémon World Championships, 20

Pokémon X and *Y*, 13

raids, 19

role-playing games, 6

sales, 16

smartphones, 16, 19

Tajiri, Satoshi, 8

timeline, 15

trade, 6, 7, 12, 18

trading cards, 20, 21

train, 6

trainers, 17, 20

TV shows, 20

United States, 6, 10

The images in this book are reproduced through the courtesy of: Fuad Suedan Diaz, front cover (Pikachu); Kieran Downs, front cover (*Pokemon Scarlet*); Illia Vakulko, p. 3; SrideeStudio, p. 4; Gabriel Hilger, pp. 4-5, 6-7, 12-13 (*Pokémon Diamond*), 14 (*Pokémon Sword, Pokémon Violet*), 15 (2019), 18-19; Heathers, p. 7 (Bulbasaur, Charmander, Squirtle); Kyodo News/ Newscom, p. 8 (Satoshi Tajiri); BugWarp/ Wikipedia, p. 8 (Pocket Monsters); Dado Photos, p. 9 (Game Boy); Game Freak Nintendo/ Wikipedia, pp. 9 (Game Freak logo), 10 (*Pokémon Red* screenshot); Cember Tech, p. 10 (Game Boy); Michel Bussieres, p. 10 (*Pokémon Red* cartridge); RG-vc, p. 11 (Game Boy Color); Marti Bug Catcher, p. 11 (a lot of Pokémon); Pe3k, p. 13 (*Pokémon X*); WildSnap, p. 15 (1996); John Hanson Pye, p. 15 (1998); Brian Hartnett/ Alamy, p. 15 (2006); Sadie Mantell, p. 15 (2022); enchanted_fairy, pp. 16-17; Wachiwit, p. 19 (on the go); Manuel Balce Ceneta/ AP Images, p. 20; Album/ Alamy, pp. 20-21; A Moment Stopped, p. 21 (trading cards); DarkBarrios/ Alamy, p. 23.